VETERAN MOTOR CARS

Steve Lanham

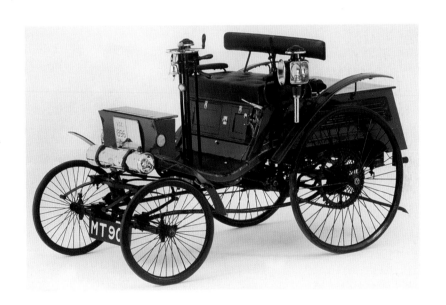

SHIRE PUBLICATIONS
Bloomsbury Publishing Plc
PO Box 883, Oxford, OX1 9PL, UK
1385 Broadway, 5th Floor, New York, NY 10018, USA

E-mail: shire@bloomsbury.com
www.shirebooks.co.uk

SHIRE is a trademark of Osprey Publishing Ltd

First published in Great Britain in 2020

A catalogue record for this book is available from the British Library.

ISBN: PB 978 1 78442 420 6

 Ebook 978 1 78442 421 3

 Epdf 978 1 78442 418 3

 XML 978 1 78442 419 0

20 21 22 23 24   10 9 8 7 6 5 4 3 2 1

Typeset by PDQ Digital Media Solutions, Bungay, UK

Printed and bound in India by Replika Press Private Ltd.

COVER IMAGE

Front cover: A 1903 De Dion Bouton Model Q. (Motoring Picture Library). Back cover image: A brass bulb horn (Motoring Picture Library).

TITLE PAGE IMAGE

The prototype Arnold Dog Cart, entered into the 1896 'Emancipation Run'. The Arnold Motor Carriage Company had acquired the rights to build Benz motor cars under licence; twelve were built in total and two survive today.

ACKNOWLEDGEMENTS

All images kindly supplied by Jon Day at the Motoring Picture Library, Beaulieu. Special thanks to Patrick Collins at the National Motor Museum Trust Reference Library.

CONTENTS

INTRODUCTION

CARS OF THE modern era follow tried-and-tested formulas in design, aerodynamics and body styling and, in a cut-throat automotive market, manufacturers do all they can to avoid producing new cars that prove unreliable in the short term. But it has taken more than a century for these standards to be established, and the development of the veteran car represents a bygone age that seems alien to today's motorist.

It was no quick and easy transition from horse-drawn to horseless carriage. If a Victorian traveller wanted to take a journey of any considerable distance, he or she would

An 1897 Dunkley
dos-à-dos
gas-powered
diamond-formation
four-wheeler.

A 1900
Clément-Panhard
automobile.

probably have chosen to go by rail. Cross-country highways did not receive the level of maintenance we demand today. The railways, on the other hand, were smooth and rapid, and, particularly for those in high society, had novelty appeal as the latest thing. As the days of the stagecoach were nearing an end, the tentacles of the rail network gradually spread to serve as many areas of Britain as possible, terrain permitting.

So, when a faster and more dependable replacement to equine motive power appeared on the roads, the public were less inclined to welcome the new technology. There was a widespread mistrust of the motor car throughout the population, and predominantly among country folk who had seen a threat to their jobs ever since the introduction of the steam engine.

Those most concerned and affected by the new breed of 'autocarists' who owned and developed the new vehicles held protests and lobbied the most sympathetic Members of Parliament (particularly those who championed the railways), and laws were implemented to restrict vehicle size, movement and operation. Nevertheless, determined inventors who could see that the future of transportation for individuals by road lay in the motor car remained undeterred in their endeavours to create a viable alternative to the horse-drawn carriage.

THE PIONEERS

A model of
Nicolas-Joseph
Cugnot's
1769 *fardier
à vapeur,* one
of the earliest
self-propelled
land vehicles.

IT SEEMS QUITE implausible now, but centuries before the
motor car first took to the roads of the world, gifted and
visionary inventors had already constructed self-propelled
vehicles in an attempt to replace the age-old horse-drawn
carriage. A Greek mathematician named Heron of Alexandria
made steam engines and powered carts as early as the first
century AD. In the 1670s, it is said that the emperor of China
was entertained by a demonstration from Flemish Jesuit
missionary, Father Ferdinand Verbiest, who allegedly showed
how a steam turbine could successfully propel a miniature
vehicle. In the late eighteenth century, Nicolas-Joseph
Cugnot constructed the *fardier à vapeur,* a front-wheel-drive,
three-wheeled steam carriage designed to transport heavy
artillery equipment. Extensive trials proved it to be too slow,
unreliable and unwieldy for any practical use. Nevertheless,
the *fardier à vapeur* is today regarded as the first full-size

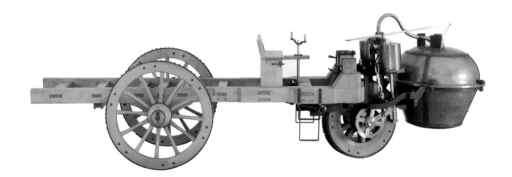

A drawing of Goldsworthy Gurney's steam carriage which ran from London to Bath in 1829.

vehicle operated by any form of self-propulsion, and it set a precedent for subsequent innovators to follow and gradually develop. However, none of these ideas were taken seriously until the steam engine had become a refined and vastly improved form of motive power.

In 1801, Cornish mining engineer Richard Trevithick built a carriage called *Puffing Devil* that featured a high-pressure steam engine. It demonstrated its capabilities on Christmas Eve that year, when, with six passengers, it made a triumphant ascent of Camborne Hill, notoriously difficult by horse and carriage, before continuing on to the village of Beacon, just over a mile away. The event had been witnessed by a young visionary, Goldsworthy Gurney, who dedicated the next twenty years to creating a passenger-carrying vehicle of his own design. He was not without competition and, during the 1820s, the press would regularly report on both Gurney's achievements and those of Walter Hancock of Marlborough in their attempts to build a successful cross-country omnibus. Hancock's well-conceived vehicle displayed advanced features for the day and was, for a short time, used by the London & Paddington Steam Carriage Company, before Hancock broke away to run an independent service.

The *Hippomobile*,
built in 1860 by
Belgian engineer
Jean Joseph
Étienne Lenoir.

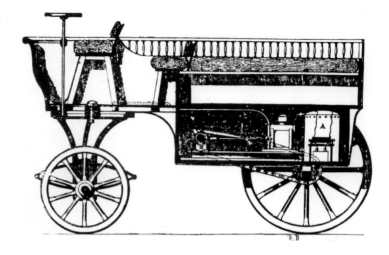

Gurney's steam carriage made a momentous return journey from London to Bath in July 1829, but encountered problems from those populating the route who saw this new form of mechanisation as a possible future threat to employment. As the carriage passed through the Wiltshire town of Melksham, local residents hurled stones, injuring the vehicle's hapless stoker in the process.

Using a steam engine in a road locomotive had a number of disadvantages, however. It typically required a crew of at least two to drive, stoke the fire and steer, and generally keep an eye on the road for any developing hazards. From cold, the fire could take well over an hour to heat the water in the boiler in order to create sufficient steam pressure to maintain a reciprocal movement of the piston or pistons within the cylinders. And during a severe winter, that water might turn to ice thus taking even longer to heat up. Steam power worked well on the railways, with a single locomotive capable of pulling an enormous load; but a steam engine in a proportionately light road vehicle transporting only a small party of travellers proved something of an encumbrance.

Coal and hydrogen-gas engines had been in development for many years and, as stationary units, were used to drive pumps or line shafts in mills and factories. There had been some experimentation with gas engines in vehicles, notably the 1807 charette built by François Isaac de Rivaz, but it was not until 1859 that a commercially successful internal combustion gas engine was produced. Belgian engineer Jean Joseph Étienne Lenoir was granted a patent for his invention and used the engine in his small carriage of 1860. Three years later, Lenoir's three-wheeled *Hippomobile* journeyed 7 miles from Paris to Joinville-le-Pont and back, in around three hours. Although very quiet, the engine was primitive, not particularly powerful and, in reality, still only an adaptation of the steam engine. In 1870, German inventor Siegfried Marcus completed his cart now widely recognised as the first vehicle to feature a simple petrol engine.

In 1876, after fifteen years of experimentation, fellow German Nikolaus Otto unveiled the first fully functioning four-stroke engine. Referred to today as the 'Otto cycle', its operation comprised an initial downward stroke of the piston drawing a coal-gas and air mixture into the cylinder, an upward stroke compressing the mixture ignited by a

Gottlieb Daimler, one of the early automotive manufacturers. This photograph was taken in 1900.

A replica of
Daimler and
Maybach's 1885
motorcycle.
Also known as
the Reitwagen
(or 'riding car'),
the original was
destroyed in a
fire in 1903.

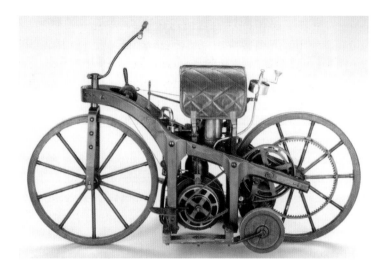

timed flame (much later, a spark), the resulting explosion forcing a second downward or power stroke, and the exhaust produced from that explosion expelled from the cylinder with a second upward stroke of the piston. It was revolutionary in its ingenuity, and a concept that stood the test of time and formed the basis of all subsequent four-stroke engines. At last, the world had a realistic alternative to steam. But Otto was not interested in modes of transport; instead, his company, Gasmotorenfabrik Deutz, started selling production units (eventually numbering over 50,000) as stationary engines.

One of Otto's employees, however, could see all too well the potential of a four-stroke engine as motive power for a horseless carriage. Gottlieb Daimler had descended from a family of bakers, but chose to hone his mechanical and technical skills training, first as a gunsmith and then at the railway engineering firm of André Koechlin & Cie. in Mulhouse, in French Alsace. While in Mulhouse, Daimler was tasked with the construction of carriages and locomotives, but his real interest lay in the advances with the internal combustion engine that were taking place elsewhere in Europe.

In 1860, Daimler resigned from the company and took a trip to Paris to view the gas engines being manufactured by Lenoir. Enthused by what he saw, he spent the next few years gaining experience with various engineering companies in Britain and Germany. During that time, he became friends with future partner Wilhelm Maybach, and in 1872, they both decided to join Otto's Gasmotorenfabrik Deutz, with Daimler appointed technical director. The relationship between Otto and Daimler seems to have been a difficult one, however, and they regularly disagreed on various aspects of production. Daimler was of the view that the company should look to the production of engines for horseless carriages, but this idea was

This Cannstatt Daimler of 1898 illustrates well how car manufacturers in the earliest years of motoring typically took design cues from vehicles of the horse drawn age.

A replica of the
954cc three-
wheeler built
by Karl Benz in
1886.

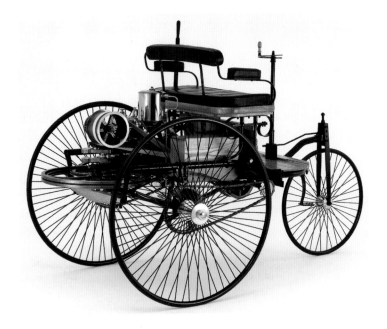

dismissed by Otto. Disillusioned by his boss's lack of foresight, Daimler resigned, with Maybach following suit soon after.

Daimler and Maybach decided to set up a workshop in Cannstatt (now called Bad Cannstatt) on the outskirts of Stuttgart, and within four years had put together a neat four-stroke engine of their own. Testing was carried out on what could now be described as the world's first motorcycle, and after satisfactory test results a four-wheeler was constructed for evaluation trials. Buoyed by further success, Daimler and Maybach opened a purpose-built factory in Cannstatt, producing power units for various applications including cars, boats, trams and railcars.

At about the same time, another German, Karl Benz, was independently striving to build a commercially viable horseless carriage. Benz's early career path was not unlike Daimler's. He started off as a clock repairer prior to joining the Maschinenbau-Gesellschaft Karlsruhe in 1866 before setting up his own machining business in Mannheim, where he could indulge his passion for the internal combustion engine. By 1879, he had successfully run a two-stroke unit and was looking for financial backing to go into vehicle production. Like Daimler, however, Benz was unable to garner the support of his business partners, who did not share his vision. Exasperated by their shortsightedness, Benz found new investors and started up Benz & Cie., Rheinische Gasmotoren-Fabrik. He now had the freedom to investigate the construction of a car, featuring a reliable and powerful engine, that could potentially be sold to the public.

An 1888 example of the Benz three-wheeler that the manufacturer's Paris-based agent, Émile Roger, was marketing under the Roger name.

By 1886, a three-wheeler with a 954cc single-cylinder four-stroke engine mounted in a purpose-built tubular frame was being tested at his Mannheim factory. With rudimentary steering to the single front wheel and simple clutch control, it was a very different contraption to the one Daimler and Maybach had trialled. Yet its performance was pleasing, and small-scale production of an improved and more powerful version began in 1888, alongside the company's main concern of stationary engines. That year, Émile Roger, a Paris-based agent for Benz & Cie. was so impressed when he saw one of the cars on show at the Munich Engineering Exposition that he bought an example as something of an advertising gimmick to support his stationary engine sales. Benz must have been delighted with this publicity, especially when his business received nearly seventy further orders for his three-wheeler.

Previous attempts by those endeavouring to build a successful alternative to the horse and cart had often been speculative and ill-conceived, and had resulted in experimental one-off prototypes. Benz and Daimler had finally achieved the ambition of many of their forebears by setting up the first companies to go into serious car production.

FROM HORSE-DRAWN CARRIAGE TO HORSELESS CARRIAGE

ONCE IT WAS realised that a dependable form of self-propelled road transport could be built, inventors looked to the horse-drawn vehicle for design inspiration. Steering was via a pivoting axle at the front, but operated using a tiller (the first known application of a steering wheel was on a Panhard-Levassor 4hp driven by Alfred Vacheron during the 1894 Paris–Rouen race). When it came to braking, manufacturers employed methods already used on traction engines. Wooden blocks, applied via a lever or screw gear directly to the surface of solid rear tyres by a quick-witted driver or passenger could help prevent a runaway situation – four-wheel braking was unheard of and was not a regular feature until just before the First World War. Chocks under the wheels, a drop-down spike embedded into the road, or even a land anchor were, for the Victorian motorist, suitable types of parking brake. Employing traditional coachmakers to craft the bodywork and frames meant the cars proved top-heavy and cumbersome in performance. It was not until the turn of the century when manufacturers chose to build their vehicles using spoked wheels and, more importantly, the sort of tubular frames already being used in a growing bicycle industry that a lighter and nimbler form of vehicle started to become commonplace on the highways.

There were many categories of horse-drawn carriage, and terms such as 'coupé', 'phaéton', 'brougham' and 'landaulet' were adopted for the different motor-car body styles to

OPPOSITE
Bersey electric cabs were once a common sight in London and by 1900, seventy-five were in operation around the streets of the capital. This one dates from 1897.

A 1903 Georges Richard coupé passes through Marble Arch on the 2005 Brighton Veteran Car Run.

identify one from another, once serious production had begun. The Victoria, for example, was traditionally a large, open four-wheeled carriage, the driver sitting high up at the front in order to gain a good view of the road over the heads of the two leading horses, while four occupants sat behind him, in pairs face to face, (or vis-à-vis). Protection against the elements came in the form of a leather canopy over a wooden frame which could be raised or lowered depending on the weather conditions. The Victoria electric car developed by Walter Bersey epitomised the horseless carriage, and to those familiar with the horse-drawn Victoria must have been a disconcerting sight, quietly trundling along devoid of any horse out front!

Bersey's London-based engineering business had built cars powered by twin electric motors since 1895 but later

An 1899 Madelvic brougham five-wheeler, with electric drive to the centre wheel.

turned its attention to taxis. By 1900, seventy-five Bersey electric cabs were operating in the capital. The term 'cab' is a derivation of 'cabriolet', a two-wheeled vehicle pulled by a single horse once preferred by Hackney carriage firms in London and many other cities. The year 1897 saw the introduction of the taximeter, a mechanical device for accurately measuring the fare payable by cab passengers according to distance travelled; and, in time, these vehicles became colloquially known as 'taxicabs'.

This Daimler Grafton Phaeton is the oldest surviving Coventry-built Daimler, dating from 1897, and is now preserved as part of The Jaguar Heritage Trust.

Both horse-drawn and motor 'wagonettes' were designed with ease of access in mind, and were often used on bus services, for example, transferring travellers from a railway station to a nearby hotel. The front seats would be taken by the driver and a passenger, while the rear compartment, entered via steps and a door at the very back of the vehicle, could hold four to six people on longitudinal benches each side, facing inwards. Shooting brakes were wagonettes built specifically for game hunters and often numbered among the vehicle fleets of many stately homes and estates. They were appointed with gun racks and hooks for the hunted game birds. The word 'brake' (sometimes 'break') refers to a very basic form of cart originally used for training a horse, helping them to become accustomed to pulling a carriage (as in 'breaking it in').

A much smaller vehicle used for hunting parties was the dog cart, so called as it featured a ventilated box for carrying gun dogs. Horse-drawn dog carts were typically two-seaters, the rear occupant riding back to back (or dos-à-dos) with the driver, but the name was also used for motorised vehicles

A 1902 Arrol-Johnston dog cart on the 2005 London to Brighton Veteran Car Run. This type took its design cues from a horse-drawn hunting vehicle where gun dogs would be carried in a compartment below the dos-à-dos (back to back) seating.

that could accommodate four or more persons seated in a similar fashion.

Buggies, featuring large diameter wheels, were better suited for the often deep-rutted and flooded highways of the American plains and the Australian outback. In Europe, there had been regionalised programmes of road improvement for the best part of two hundred years, and cycle-type wheels could be used to a greater extent. Early motorcycles, tricycles and quadricycles, constructed with small engines in tubular frames, led to the introduction of cheap single or dual-seat vehicles called 'cyclecars' or 'voiturettes'.

As a motorised vehicle, the buckboard was the simplest form of passenger car, sometimes a light car or cyclecar, and more often a two-seater of very rudimentary design with a flat bed at the back for carrying goods – very much the forerunner of the pickup. 'Buckboard' was formerly the term given to a simple four-wheeled, single horse-drawn vehicle popular in the United States. It took its name from the driver's footrest, a flat board that protected the occupants in case the horse bucked and kicked back. The buckboard also stopped muck

The 1893 Duryea 4hp buggy represented a type of high-wheeler commonly seen especially in parts of North America designed to cope with deep-rutted and flooded roads.

and grit being thrown up over the driver and his passengers from the action of the horses' hooves, thus providing some form of protection, particularly during inclement weather. This feature was later referred to as a 'dashboard' and adopted by various car manufacturers, particularly in the States, including the company producing the Oldsmobile – the very first automotive manufacturer to set up business in heart of America's motor industry, Detroit.

Ransom Eli Olds had already constructed two self-propelled steam vehicles at his father's mechanical workshop in Lansing, Michigan, before developing an internal combustion engine with his colleague, Madison Bates. A patent was granted in 1897, and production began with some of his engines installed into road vehicles. At Detroit railroad station later that year, a chance meeting with copper-mining magnate Samuel L. Smith led to the establishment of the Olds Motor Vehicle Company, with Smith financing the lion's share. Various

prototype models of large town cars and small light vehicles were completed, one of them being a two-seater runabout featuring a curved dashboard, and deemed the most likely candidate for lucrative sales. Before any assembly could commence, however, the factory burned to the

Light cars or cyclecars were often known as 'voiturettes'. The word 'voiturette' had been adopted by the Bollee firm for its diminutive vehicle so the 1899 Decauville 3½hp illustrated here was marketed as the 'voiturelle'.

ground. The company was rebranded the Olds Motor Works and relocated back to Lansing with the prototype runabout the only item saved from the blaze. Production began in earnest from new premises and, between 1901 and the end of 1904, over 12,000 examples of this popular little model were sold. In 1904, Ransom Eli Olds resigned from the company and set up a new concern under the name Reo.

In time, the dashboard became the ideal location for controls and instrumentation on all cars. Repositioned behind the engine, it acted as a wind break as well as a barrier against the not uncommon possibility of engine fire! But it was the Panhard company, and its 'système Panhard' of 1896 which really set the standard for the general layout of subsequent motor cars.

The French automobile manufacturer Panhard et Levassor can trace its origins back to carriage builder Adrien Panhard, who founded his firm Prieur in Paris in the 1830s. Adrien's son, René, and Émile Levassor, who had become friends at the same engineering school, took great interest in Lenoir's gas engines while running a business making industrial woodworking machinery. Further investigations brought them into contact with Gottlieb Daimler and the four-stroke engines being made by his Stuttgart works. René and Émile formed Société Panhard et Levassor in 1886 and in 1889 agreed to make Daimler engines under licence for use in Peugeot cars. A year later, Levassor commissioned one of his own staff to fabricate a complete car in their factory to evaluate the practicalities of going into whole car production. It was fitted with a 921cc V-twin engine producing 1½hp, neatly mounted between a back-to-back seating arrangement.

A second car, this time with the engine positioned further to the rear, was built in 1891. Both cars proved their worth during testing although Levassor had already seen where improvements could be made. He realised that if the engine was located forward of the driver and above the front wheels, it not only reduced vibration but also gave positivity to the steering. In doing so, the passenger area could now be built lower in the frame, thus improving the centre of balance.

Further weight reduction was achieved when Daimler's small but equally powerful 1,201cc Phoenix engine was introduced in 1896; this, combined with Levassor's all-enclosed sliding gearbox, gave the directors confidence that they had a reliable and viable vehicle, suitable for production. Panhard et Levassor perfected the in-line layout of – from the front of the car – radiator ahead of the engine and above the front steering axle, gearbox to transmission driving the rear wheels; the driver and passengers sat behind the engine separated by a dashboard. Today the same format is used by all motoring manufacturers and referred to as '*système* Panhard'.

A 1902 Oldsmobile Runabout showing the beautifully sculpted footboard that gave this type its 'curved-dash' name.

OVERLEAF
A wagonette type built in 1899 by one of the pioneering motor manufacturers, Panhard et Levassor. Wagonettes were popular with hoteliers for transporting their guests to and from railway stations.

FROM BACKSTREET WORKSHOP TO HOUSEHOLD NAME

WHILE THE LIKES of Benz and Daimler were perfecting their engines and setting up factories to build production cars, there were also hundreds of workshops and inventive cottage industries throughout Europe, tinkering away in the hope of becoming worthy competitors. For the most part, these were mere forays into mechanical invention and experimentation, and a great number of enterprises fell by the wayside, either through lack of finances, lack of interest or unreliability. But the firms that managed to create quality and saleable products were largely built on a combination of accomplished engineering and superior business acumen. Eventually a few would become household names and in

The Benz Velo was one of the success stories of the period. Designed by a mechanical genius, it proved consistently reliable and became a popular seller, marketed not only by Benz, but also in various guises when assembled under licence by other firms.

time form the basis of today's motoring conglomerates.

Austrian businessman Emil Jellinek had by the turn of the century established an agency representing Daimler on the south coast of France. Jellinek's relationship with Gottlieb Daimler was not an easy one, and he was particularly critical of the instability of Daimler's cars at high speed. After a fatal crash at the 1900 La Turbie Hillclimb race, he recommended an all-new car with a lower centre of gravity, and as an incentive promised to buy thirty-six examples on condition that he could sell them under a brand named after his young daughter, Mercédès. In 1901, Mercedes cars not only dominated motor racing but also cashed in on the publicity, securing lucrative sales. By 1903, an extensive range of Mercedes luxury cars was emerging from a purpose-built factory in Stuttgart.

Once an engine had been tested and proven dependable, it was often made available as an off-the-shelf proprietary unit, exported to manufacturers worldwide to power their own-design autocars. Alternatively, some companies built the same engines on home soil but under licence, and many well-known firms were established during the period in this way. Benz and De Dion-Bouton were the leading engine suppliers in Europe and provided motor units to the likes of Argyll, Arnold, Humber, Renault and Sunbeam until such organisations had accrued enough expertise to build their own engines.

During the mid-1800s, the Midlands was very much the centre of bicycle production in Britain, and towards the end of the century, a number of factories around Birmingham and

Renault was one of the earlier manufacturers that understood the importance of reliable engineering, effective marketing and good business acumen. This diminutive 1¾hp model was built in 1899 at its Billancourt factory on the outskirts of Paris.

Many European motor manufacturers utilised engines supplied by De Dion Bouton to provide power for their vehicles. But the Paris-based company was an established car maker in its own right as illustrated by the smart little 6hp Model Q of 1903.

Coventry decided to branch out and turn their hand to building motorcycles and cars. Both Ariel and Royal Enfield launched a line of light vehicles and looked to De Dion-Bouton for a source of engines. Their tricycles and quadricycles were operated by foot pedals and hand controls located on the handlebars, and could be bought with passenger trailer attachments, or fitted with a wicker seat positioned forward of the rider. They were cheap to run and relatively cheap to buy, allowing a greater sector of the population, especially those of lesser means, to enjoy the freedom of motorised transport that had, for many years, only been the preserve of the upper classes.

There were, however, many engineers who had enough confidence and understanding to create their own internal combustion engines, and it was their innovative ideas that generated the most interest in the motoring press.

Frederick Lanchester, for example, is regarded as one of the most innovative engineers of his time and was responsible for many concepts still regarded as fundamental in the automotive industry today. Lanchester learned his trade through working for the Forward Gas Engine Company of Birmingham, but started to develop an interest in motoring when he saw a Benz on show at the 1889 Paris Exhibition.

In four years, he had not only set up his own engineering works but built his first single-cylinder engine. In 1896, he and his brother, George, test-drove a complete car before rebuilding it with an improved twin-cylinder horizontally opposed unit and three-speed gearbox, and replaced the chain with a worm gear final drive. Later an ingenious system of braking was introduced which operated directly on the worm gear and, in 1902, the Lanchester Engine Company added a water-cooled model to its range. By the end of 1904, the catalogue offered seven different models including the company's first four-cylinder car.

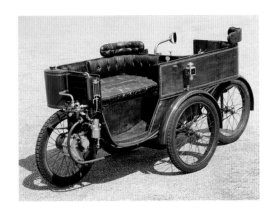

The rather unorthodox 1902 Sunbeam Mabley 2¾hp diamond-formation four-wheeler was one such vehicle that benefited from a De Dion Bouton engine. Although it was located at the front of the vehicle, it powered the central two wheels via belts and a chain.

Another success story was that of Wolseley. Initially founded in Australia as the Wolseley Sheep Shearing Machine Company, Wolseley opened its first factory in Birmingham in 1889 to build cars under the directorship of one Herbert Austin. The company entered two cars in the Thousand Mile Trial of 1900 and should have profited from the publicity their success attracted, but it was not until it was taken over by armaments manufacturer Vickers, Sons and Maxim that production could commence. For the first two years, Wolseleys featured horizontal engines giving them a low slung and attractive appearance. They should have been ideal vehicles for competitive events but their performances in European races never lived up to expectation. In 1903, Vickers bought the Coventry firm Siddeley and started building Wolseleys with vertical engines under the influence of Siddeley's chief engineer, John Davenport. By then, Herbert Austin had left to establish a marque under his own name, later producing some of Britain's most iconic cars including the Austin 7, the Cambridge and the Issigonis-designed Mini.

An 1898 Ariel tricycle. This manufacturer initially built De Dion Bouton vehicles under licence but was soon marketing its own designs.

Rover started life in 1877 as Starley and Sutton, yet another bicycle manufacturer from Coventry. In 1885, John Kemp Starley unveiled his 'Rover Safety Bicycle', whose revolutionary design consisted of equal diameter wheels and a chain drive to a rear sprocket. It completely changed the sport of cycling and superseded the age-old penny-farthing, also known as an 'ordinary'. In 1896, the business was renamed the Rover Cycle Company, and in 1903, it started building a prototype motor car under the guidance of former Daimler engineer Edmund Lewis. This was very much a vehicle designed from the ground up but constructed of a tubular frame utilising the skills of their bicycle factory workers. Even the 1,327cc single-cylinder engine had been conceived in the Rover drawing office and, by the end of 1904, an 8hp production model was on sale.

Across the Atlantic, Ford had opened its production campaign with the Model A. It came seven years after Henry

A 1902 Lanchester alongside a 1900 Serpollet steam car – contemporary rivals at a time when petrol, steam and electric were still vying for supremacy as the most suitable form of automotive power.

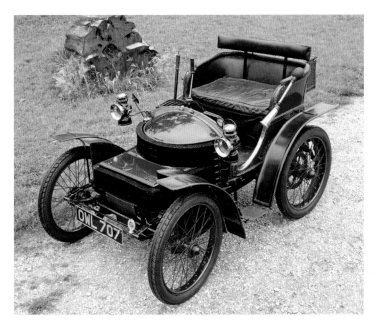

An 1899 Wolseley similar to the one Herbert Austin drove in the Thousand Mile Trial.

Specifically designed to appeal to the masses, the Ford Model A was sold at the budget end of the market. It was nevertheless an attractive automobile and instrumental in making the Ford Motor Company one of the fastest expanding car manufacturers of its day. This example dates from 1903.

Ford completed his first car in 1896, cobbled together from whatever spare parts he could lay his hands on at his then employer, the Edison Illuminating Company, Detroit. The Model A was a neat little runabout featuring a Dodge Brothers engine mounted in a body outsourced to a local coachmaker. It was specifically built with cost in mind as Ford could see a huge untapped market in the lower classes, an ethos that paid huge dividends in the fortunes of the company. By 1904, it had sold enough examples of the A to finance a brand-new factory, and within twelve months, the Ford Motor Company not only had a staff of 300 but was producing more vehicles per day than any other car manufacturer in the world.

A CHANGING LANDSCAPE

B Y THE EARLY 1800s, and as a direct result of the Industrial Revolution, British cities such as London, Birmingham, Liverpool, and Manchester had developed into vast centres of manufacture. The web of canals, and later the railways, allowed rapid transportation of goods to a wider customer base, and in return brought coal in to fuel the stationary steam engines that powered the factories, mills, tanneries and furnaces. Wealthy businessmen and landowners cashed in on the growth with little concern for the environmental damage this caused or the health and wellbeing of the common man.

Westminster Bridge in London, in the days before motorised vehicles.

A 1902 Argyll
8hp Tonneau,
with driver and
front passenger
kitted out with
dust goggles.

The air was thick with the stench of sulphur and the sky darkened by acrid smoke belching from the chimneys, their soot-laden fallout covering houses and shops in a filthy grime. As many operations ran day and night, a constant noise reverberated out to neighbouring districts, and families housed within commuting distance would suffer illnesses that were exacerbated by their atrocious living conditions. Yet populations grew, and the draw of potential employment attracted more people in from the countryside. Land was at a premium and streets off main thoroughfares had developed haphazardly into narrow alleyways and lanes.

It took a long time for authorities to realise that the future of rapid transit across a built-up area lay in mechanised form, be it trams, buses or cars. It was not until the very end of the nineteenth century that wider roads allowing the passing and parking of vehicles were incorporated into town planning. Nevertheless, there had at least been some effort made to reduce congestion in Britain's great industrial conurbations – driving on the left on certain roads, especially in London, was decreed from the mid-1700s, and by 1835, that rule was implemented throughout the country.

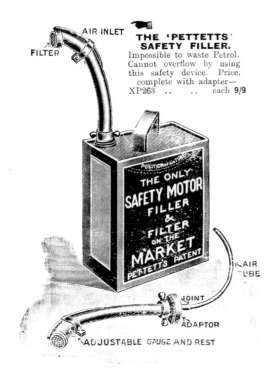

THE 'PETTETTS'
SAFETY FILLER.
Impossible to waste Petrol.
Cannot overflow by using
this safety device. Price,
complete with adapter—
XP263 .. .. each 9/9

An advertisement for a fuel pourer showing the type of cans early motorists used to fill their cars with petrol.

In the days before passenger and goods services by rail, travellers and itinerant vendors would cross the country by horse, or horse-drawn vehicle and, at regular intervals, pause at a coaching inn. Such establishments would offer a place to dine, drink, sleep and generally recover ahead of the next day's journey. Carriages would be housed in covered sheds, and stables would provide a well-earned rest for the horses. With the coming of the railways, those looking to make a lengthy trip favoured the smoother, quicker rail option over the rutted, dusty and often flooded roads. The public house soon fell out of favour as an overnight stopover, and looked to the local population of farm or factory workers for custom. Much larger hotels were constructed at railway stations, junctions and termini, as well as in mountainous and seaside resorts where those rich enough could rest and recuperate away from their day-to-day work. But as the autocar began establishing itself as a reliable form of road transport, the traditional coaching inn had a revival, welcoming touring owners and enthusiasts. Stables and sheds were gradually converted into motor garages, and outhouses or lofts that had previously served to temporarily house saddles, tackle and hay, would often be upgraded into accommodation for the long-suffering chauffeurs and drivers.

In 1919, the Automobile Association opened the first purpose-built petrol station at Aldermaston in Berkshire.

There were still very few cars on the road and, up until that time, owners of automobiles had to rely on purchasing petrol from ironmongers, hardware stores and apothecaries. In the late-Victorian era, petrol was delivered to the retailers by 'lurry' (horse-drawn wagon) and distributed in cans. For the autocarist, locating a shop that sold appropriate fuel would have added to the level of organisation involved prior to taking a journey of any considerable distance.

Blacksmiths' forges also had to adapt to the new technology. Traditionally attending the needs of the horse-and-carriage owner, they were increasingly accepting work from autocarists whose vehicles required regular servicing, repair and maintenance. Breakdowns were common, attributed not only to the somewhat experimental and fragile nature of the vehicle itself but, more often than not, due to the atrocious state of the roads.

Cycle shops would have been able to undertake minor car repairs. This one dates to the mid-1890s.

For centuries, carriageways had been dusty in summer and muddy affairs during inclement weather, with unsurfaced or poorly surfaced roads suffering constant erosion as a result of the passing of horse-drawn carriages and goods wagons; in many cases, these roads were quite unsuitable for the arrival of the motor car. In order to finance the making, repairing and maintaining of highways, bridges and drainage ditches, turnpike trusts were founded in Britain from the seventeenth century onwards. Money was collected from travellers and bulk carriers via tollgates located on major thoroughfares which was used to pay for the roads' upkeep, and the scheme was such a success that countries around the globe adopted the idea. The turnpike trustees were landowners, merchants and members of the clergy, and a team of administrators officiated over proceedings. In time, these powers would be consolidated into county and borough councils as a result of the 1888 Local Government Act.

While working for the Bristol Turnpike Trust, a surveyor called John Loudoun McAdam introduced a system of

A 1901 New Orleans under repair in a blacksmith's shop. The New Orleans company did not hail from the United States, but in fact manufactured their vehicles out of a factory in Twickenham, Middlesex, located on Orleans Road – hence the name.

road-making that revolutionised the way highways are built worldwide. His idea was to lay beds of gravel on top of hard-core rock, with a smooth top surface of small stones formed into a curve or camber to direct rainwater to the edge of the road and into ditches either side.

A road being sprayed with westrumite oil mixture to limit dust clouds.

But the greatest advance to improving the comfort of road-going passengers was the invention of the pneumatic tyre. Solid tyres, often made from iron, steel or rubber, had already been used to prevent the outer rim of a wooden wheel from splintering. The introduction of a cushion of air between wheel and road dramatically reduced the bumps and jostling effect of an uneven surface. In 1839, Charles Goodyear discovered a way of vulcanising rubber – hardening the material for greater durability – and, within seven years, Scottish inventor Robert Thomson had patented a pneumatic tyre using the process.

But it was not until 1887 and in Belfast, that fellow Scot, John Boyd Dunlop, managed to perfect the idea. He fitted three pneumatic tyres to his son's tricycle as he envisaged it would roll with greater ease over the cobbled streets than with its usual solid rims. The results were startling, and two years later, a racing bicycle fitted with Dunlop's tyres and ridden by Willie Hume, captain of the Belfast Cruisers' Cycling Club, won four events in Belfast, and three out of four in Liverpool. One spectator was Harvey Du Cros, president of the Irish Cyclists' Association. So impressed was Du Cros with the difference in speed between Hume and the other competitors that he proposed a new business venture with Dunlop that would culminate in the founding of the Dunlop Pneumatic Tyre Company. In 1896, they had divisions not only in Coventry, the centre of British bicycle and motoring manufacture, but factories worldwide too. By then, however, there were also a number of rival tyre producers including Goodyear, Michelin and Palmer.

An 1896 Pennington Autocar sporting pneumatic tyres. The front two passengers are Mr and Mrs Edward Joel Pennington.

ACCESSORIES FOR THE AUTOCARIST

COMPLETING A JOURNEY of any length is generally taken for granted today but, in the era of the horse-drawn carriage, even short excursions from village to village would prove something of an adventure, fraught with all manner of hazards, dangers and the occasional unsavoury character to hamper progress. Once the automobile became a familiar sight on the roads of the world, the fragility of its construction and mechanical unreliability simply added to the issues. Whether or not a motorist would reach their destination was often in the lap of the gods. To increase any chances of success, they would take with them an array of essential spare parts and a full toolkit as blacksmiths' shops were few and far between, and service stations, placed at regular intervals, were most certainly still a thing of the dim and distant future. Spark plugs, lubricating oil, spanners, screwdrivers and specialist tools for performing particular tasks such as changing a tyre might all

Turn-of-the-century motoring fashion, featuring a passenger blanket and waterproofs.

be packed before setting off from home, and if a container of water had not been included, then a stop-off next to a stream could very well be called for to replenish a boiling radiator.

For an overnight stay, clothes would be carried in travel trunks, some specially designed to compliment the general

A lady, appropriately attired for a day's motoring, stands in front of a 1903 Renault. A wicker basket which might typically contain a picnic is on the side of the vehicle; any luggage would have been placed on the roof rack.

decor of a vehicle's interior. In the event of a breakdown or in case a public house or hotel could not be found by lunchtime, picnic hampers became all the rage to ensure a hungry motorist and his passengers had some form of sustenance. To celebrate the new age of motoring, ceramic firms launched a range of motoring-themed dining sets that could easily be packed into a basket, and with folding chairs stowed on board, the owner of an autocar could enjoy the delights of the countryside without forgoing his creature comforts.

And personal comfort was certainly on the minds of those who took up motoring as a pastime. A night at the opera might once have seen a lady attired in a many-layered outfit gracefully descending the steps of her horse-drawn carriage while hand in hand with a gentleman friend. For motoring, however, long dresses together with their notoriously cumbersome bustle cages proved utterly impractical, and merely exiting a car could be a challenge, with passengers required to step over an oily drive chain or grease-and-mud covered brake rodding and cables. To alleviate the situation, manufacturers introduced running boards – flat platforms which not only acted as convenient steps but, with the addition of mudguards, prevented the occupants

Protective motoring goggles and dust veils were essential accessories for the Victorian motorist before the advent of windscreens.

A 1901
De Dion-Bouton
voiturette with
the driver and
passengers
seated vis-à-vis
sharing a blanket.

from being spattered by mud and dust flung up by the wheels.
With the motor car attaining greater speeds than could ever
be sustained using a horse as motive power, those travelling by
road soon felt the cold, and it was quite obvious that alternative
apparel needed to be worn.

A driver who had traditionally controlled his vehicle by
means of reins attached to the horse's bridle and a simple
brake handle now found it necessary to operate a series of
pedals, levers and knobs, and often in quick succession. The
tailoring of waterproof coats and trousers, for example, as well
as dresses, boots and other everyday garments, had to reflect
these quite specific requirements, leading to a whole new
line of fashion items. Also available were blankets, gloves and
gauntlets, fur-lined accessories for winter warmth and, before
it was felt necessary to fit cars with windscreens, full-face
goggles and ladies' hats veiled with gauze in order to prevent
summer dust from irritating their eyes.

THE BRITISH MOTOR SYNDICATE LTD

40 HOLBORN VIADUCT E.C.

LICENSED TO THE DAIMLER MOTOR Co Lᵗᴰ AND
THE GREAT HORSELESS CARRIAGE Co Lᵗᴰ

STANLEY SHOW · 1896
AGRICULTURAL HALL.

PROMOTION, RACING AND RELIABILITY

I N THE BEGINNING, it was only the upper classes of society who could afford such a luxury as an 'autocar', or those in the middle classes who possessed a certain level of mechanical knowledge and the means to construct and adequately run such a machine. Very few of the rich had previously taken the reins of a horse and carriage when wanting to be seen out and about, and after buying a horseless carriage, many chose to advertise for a chauffeur or indeed inform their own coachman that his job title had changed! The problem was that the coachman probably had about as much technical expertise as his employer, and often had to be retrained in the art of driving.

To begin with, a chauffeur or driver had to really know the quirks, eccentricities, handling characteristics, limitations and shortcomings of his vehicle. It was a time of great experimentation, and different manufacturers chose alternative methods of steering, braking, ignition and carburation. Unlike today's cars, where a turn of the key is all it takes to fire up an engine, there was an order of procedures that needed to be followed to successfully start the Victorian-era motor. The driver had to be reasonably strong as he was expected to swing a starting handle against the counteracting forces of compression from a large piston, and with enough continuous vigour for the engine to cough into life. This, however, could go horribly wrong. If the timing was slightly out, the resulting ignition of fuel could send the engine into reverse and, with

An early poster advertising the motor show in Stanley, Durham.

it, the rotation of the starting handle. A quick-witted motorist might jump clear when this happened, but if he was not so lucky could easily sustain a broken limb. It was imperative to understand the ratios of petrol-to-air carburation, not only to start the thing, but keep it going thereafter. On many occasions, an incompetent could be found at the side of the road, sweating with exhaustion from his ineffectual attempts at getting the engine to run, simply because he had not grasped the importance of correct fuel mixture.

Plenty of those wealthy enough to own a horseless carriage were only too eager to occupy the driver's seat, and there was growing consternation at the number of autocarists who drove irresponsibly and could not properly control their vehicles. In the eyes of the public, the law, and the lawmakers, this new form of mechanised road transport was both a nuisance and a menace. In order to minimise the amount of road accidents, small motor vehicles were treated with the same level of bureaucracy as rules pertaining to traction engines.

Subsequently, the Locomotives on Highways Acts (described in the next chapter), and similar statutes in countries throughout Europe, hindered any real chance of putting an automobile (with a competent and capable driver at the helm) through its paces, without risking a fine from the local authorities. Instead, organised events were held, taking the form of races, hill climbs, reliability demonstrations and long distance tours; and it was hoped that these would simultaneously raise awareness, allay fears and improve public opinion. These events were sponsored by motor clubs, the vehicle manufacturers, businessmen looking to profit and most importantly the press – after all, daily reports from the various contests would not only make household names of the competitors (drivers and machines alike) but would, of course, help to sell thousands of newspapers to an eager and interested readership.

The first such event took place in 1894 when a trial was arranged by the newspaper *Le Petit Journal* to run between the two cities of Paris and Rouen. Of the hundred or so vehicles taking part in eight qualifying stages through the streets of the French capital, many had been entered by already well-known car manufacturers. Only twenty-one

entries managed to get through to the main trial, and on 22 July crossed the starting line at Port Maillot, before steadily making their way west towards Normandy. First to make it into Rouen was Jules Albert, Count de Dion, one of France's major advocates of motoring. Six hours and forty-eight minutes after leaving Paris, he crossed the finish line and was promptly disqualified as his six-seater De Dion, Bouton tractor and passenger trailer required two people to handle its steam engine! Next into Rouen was Albert Lemaître driving a 3hp Peugeot but, as this was not a race, the top prize of 5,000 gold francs was divided between Peugeot and Panhard et Levassor with both of their vehicles meeting the criteria of 'the competitor whose car comes closest to the ideal'. The 1894 Paris–Rouen Trial was the world's first motoring competition and after its unmitigated success, further contests were soon being advertised.

A Gautier-Wehrlé steam car taking part in the 1894 Paris-Rouen Trial. Out of twenty-one starters, it finished sixteenth.

The following year, the French capital played host to the start and also finish of a gruelling 732-mile race to Bordeaux and back. And once again, it was Panhard et Levassor and Peugeot taking the lion's share of plaudits, with Émile Levassor recording a quite magnificent time of forty-eight hours, forty-eight minutes in his 1,205cc two-seater. Second was Louis Rigoulot in a two-seater Peugeot in fifty-four hours,

An early exercise in aerodynamics was Henri Vallée's Pantoufle ('Slipper'), his entry for the 1899 Paris-St Malo Race. Finishing a highly respectable fifth, the Pantoufle had a 7,598cc horizontal four-cylinder engine with direct drive via a belt to the rear axle.

thirty-five minutes, and third, Paul Koechlin, driving a four-seater Peugeot in just under sixty hours. Koechlin received the spoils of victory, however, as the event was officially a race for four-seater cars! No doubt Levassor competed just for the publicity, and his shrewd judgment certainly paid off as it led to lucrative sales for the company.

Parisians were getting used to seeing events start from their city and witnessed subsequent races to Marseilles, Dieppe, St Malo and across the French border to Amsterdam and Berlin – every one a greater test of the reliability of each car, pushing the driver to the point of mental and physical exhaustion, and bringing excitement and an increasing element of risk ever closer to its spectators.

At last, motoring seemed to be gaining in popularity, and a following was spreading worldwide. In 1895, the British organised their first motor show called the Horseless Carriage Exhibition at Tunbridge Wells, Kent; in the same year, Americans watched the 54-mile Chicago Times-Herald Race on a snowy Thanksgiving Day, the race being won by Frank Duryea in only the second car he and his brother Charles had ever built.

The United States had a well-established railroad network connecting cities and heavily occupied regions, but because it was such a large country, it also contained huge tracts of sparsely populated land that simply could not be served by rail. In the Midwest, which contained vast areas that were mostly wilderness, the automobile proved an ideal way of getting about on the dirt roads linking settlements in the back of beyond.

Despite an apparent lack of interest in the new technology in Westminster, the British public were developing a real fascination for the motor car, even though few could ever hope to afford one. Their enthusiasm was fuelled not only by promotional spectacles but also press reports of long-distance reliability trials. Henry Sturmey (of Sturmey-Archer bicycle gear fame), who was instrumental in launching *The Autocar* magazine, decided in 1897 to take a much publicised seventeen-day trip from John O'Groats to Lands End to generate public interest. In a serialised article called *On an Autocar Through the Length and Breadth of the Land*, he described the sights, adventures and mishaps that he and his fellow traveller, Daimler engineer Richard Ashley, encountered as they arrived in each town. Often drawing a mixed crowd of the curious, the suspicious and the occasional troublemaker, his commentary on the pros and cons of late-nineteenth-century motoring proved a fascinating read.

In 1900, the Thousand Mile Trial was organised by the Automobile Club of Great Britain and Ireland (later to become the Royal Automobile Club and shortened to RAC). It was fully supported by European manufacturers who saw it as an ideal way to promote the versatility, reliability and virtues of their particular vehicles. Sixty-five cars began the tour from London on 23 April, and over the next twenty days visited Bristol in the west, Edinburgh in the north, and all major towns and cities in between before returning to the capital and the finish through Marble Arch. At various stopping points, lavish banquets were

A 1900 MMC
6hp Daimler type
two-seater at the
Thousand Mile
Trial.

John Douglas-
Scott-Montagu
at the wheel of
his 1899 Daimler
pauses during
the Paris–Ostend
Race.

laid on, interspersed with sideshows such as hill climbs, short races and exhibitions. Such events brought much-needed publicity and exposure to the masses, but news from overseas was already occupying a considerable amount of column space.

The Paris–Ostend Race of 1899 tempted Charles Rolls and John Douglas-Scott-Montagu, 2nd Baron of Beaulieu, to cross the English Channel and take part in a European motoring competition, the first time a British contingent had ever done so. On that occasion, Rolls (in only his debut race) came second in a Panhard, while Montagu, driving his own 12hp Daimler, finished third – both in the Touring Class.

Attainment of greater speed could only be realised through advances in technical development. In April 1899,

Belgian racing driver Camille Jenatzy climbed aboard *La Jamais Contente,* an electric car purpose-built for land-speed attempts with a torpedo-shaped alloy body. Jenatzy had constructed his first car only two years before and had since

specialised in the supply of electric cabs, but 'the Red Devil', as he was known due to the colour of his beard, drove to a record 105.88km/h (65.75mph), the first time a car had broken the 100km/h mark.

Camille Jenatzy in his land-speed record breaker *La Jamais Contente,* 1899.

Elsewhere, millionaire and owner of the *New York Herald,* James Gordon Bennett, Jr, offered to sponsor a cup which would be presented to the winner of the 1900 Paris–Lyons Race, the Coupe Internationale. It was the first of six trophies awarded annually to bear the Gordon Bennett name with the French Panhards dominating the first two races. But in 1902, and after a gruelling three days and 552 miles of driving, Selwyn Edge brought the prize back to Britain, having coaxed

A 1903 General 40hp racing car, built for W.G. Crombie as an entry into the Nice Speed Trials.

Camille Jenatzy's mechanic attempts to start the race-winning Mercedes 60hp at the 1903 Gordon Bennett Cup, Athy, Ireland.

his Napier across the Innsbruck finishing line in the III Coupe Internationale, the only entry to do so!

The Paris–Vienna Race saw one of the Renault brothers, Marcel, take such a commanding lead over his rivals that, when he crossed the finishing line, not even the race officials had arrived to greet him!

In July 1903, the IV Coupe Internationale was held at Athy in Ireland, competing once again for the Gordon Bennett Cup. Racing was forbidden on mainland Britain so the organisers, the Automobile Club of Great Britain and Ireland, approached Irish Members of Parliament and councillors in Kildare who were only too pleased to host such a potentially lucrative event. France, Germany and the United States entered teams to try to beat the holders, Britain, who crossed the Irish Sea with three Napiers, each symbolically painted the colour of shamrock, thereby coining the phrase 'British Racing Green'. For the first time, the course comprised a circuit using closed roads. It was laid out

The famous Napier Gordon Bennett racing cars, the first to carry British Racing Green.

over two loops in a figure of eight and required seven laps of the track, amounting to a total distance of 327 miles. With the three French cars (two Panhards and a Mors) following close behind, former land-speed record-holder Camille Jenatzy triumphed in his Mercedes, and the Gordon Bennett Cup went back to Germany.

If city-to-city events of previous years were intended to attract public and government support for open-road competition, then the Paris–Madrid Race of 1903 almost single-handedly put all that effort to waste. Organised by a coalition committee from the Automobile Club de France and the Automóvil Club Español, it was to be held over three stages, and equated to 812 miles of racing through winding streets of villages and towns, and out onto tortuous unpaved tracks in the countryside.

Early on the morning of the 24 May, 100,000 Parisians gathered against a backdrop of the beautiful Gardens of Versailles, and 224 competitors lined up for the start. These included 137 cars, thirty-three light voiturettes and fifty-four motorcycles, and each entrant was individually flagged away over the next three hours at one-minute intervals, Charles Jarrott and his 45hp De Dietrich being the first to leave. This stage took the field southwest towards the initial checkpoint at Rambouillet, but participants were experiencing difficulties even before they had left the capital, not least from the throng of spectators lining the route. With little in the way of crowd control, many spilled onto the course to get a better view, slowing progress of the racers, which in turn only exacerbated the situation.

Once away from the city, dust clouds from each passing car reduced visibility to a dangerous level. Some of the competitors sensibly reduced their speed while others took advantage and careered on at a suicidal pace. Marcel Renault, for example, had already caught up with the pacesetters some 200 miles into the race, despite having started an hour behind the leading drivers. His rapid progress was to no avail as his

car left the road and crashed at Couhé-Vérac, killing the mechanic, with the unfortunate Marcel succumbing to his injuries two days later.

Further on, Leslie Porter, driving a 50hp Wolseley, collided with a closed gate at a railway level crossing and the car caught fire. Although Porter was able to escape with minor injuries, his mechanic, trapped in the wreckage was not so lucky and perished in the inferno. In Châtellerault, a soldier was hit and lost his life attempting to rescue a child who had run into the road. The car, a Tourand, driven by Brunhot, then swerved out of control and piled into onlookers, killing one and injuring many others. While the front runners sped on, breakdowns and crashes accounted for the loss of over half of the rest of the field, and the death toll rose with the lives of another spectator and several more participants claimed during the course of the morning.

Around midday, Marcel Renault's brother Louis finally reached the end of the stage in Bordeaux, ahead of all other competitors. Jarrott's De Dietrich, and then the Mors of Fernand Gabriel, crossed the line in second and third respectively. Start times were taken into consideration and, as Gabriel's race had commenced so far down the order in 168th position, he was officially declared winner of the first stage. It was a hollow victory, paling into insignificance as the awful truth became known. News of the dead reached the French and Spanish governments who promptly called for the contest to be halted. Neither country would give permission for proceedings to continue and the remaining two stages were immediately abandoned.

Newspapers jumped on the story, sensationalising events and exaggerating the number of casualties. Nevertheless, five competitors and three spectators had died, countless people had been wounded and, in a single day, a dark cloud had descended over motor racing. An inquest apportioned blame on a combination of factors including the lack of barriers to contain the crowds, the surprising speed which some of the cars were attaining, and poor visibility due to the dust. The so-called 'Race of Death' brought to a close a chapter of European open-road city-to-city racing where there was no real way of adequately policing such long routes. It would be another twenty-four years before such an arduous event was staged again, when Italy hosted the 1927 Mille Miglia, and for the time being racing would be confined to closed circuits.

Madame du Gast aboard her De Dietrich ahead of the 1903 Paris–Madrid. Her race would end when she stopped to help another competitor injured in a crash.

THE 'EMANCIPATION ACT' AND LONDON TO BRIGHTON

As soon as the steam locomotive made its presence felt out on the road, it built quite a reputation, based not on the brilliance and innovative genius of its engineers and inventors, but as a result of the panic it generated, not least to the many horses pulling carriages up and down the country. As a form of motive power, the horse was still very much favoured, but these naturally jittery animals became easily frightened when confronted with such loud, clanking, hissing monsters. The brutal effect of the new machines on the roads also caused alarm – while the constant passing of horses' hooves was damaging to road surfaces, the weight of a traction engine could cause a road to collapse; and so local authorities were therefore generally reluctant to introduce any scheduled services which involved steam-powered road vehicles.

In 1834, the Steam Carriage Company of Scotland launched a passenger service linking Glasgow to Paisley. The vehicles consisted of a passenger compartment, a steam engine at the rear attended by a driver and stoker, and a steersman positioned on a seat at the front, guiding the vehicle via a tiller. A second carriage trailed behind with extra passenger seating and a coal bunker. The route was not as ambitious as the company owner, John Russell, had intended: his idea had been to create a rapid transit system between Glasgow and Edinburgh, but he had had to curb his plans after objections by that area's turnpike trust. Even then they were unhappy at the thought of a speeding vehicle, laden with heavy steam engine, churning up 12 miles of an already overburdened road every hour in each direction. Just four months after the first of Russell's carriages made its inaugural journey, an attempt was made to sabotage the service. A load of road-making stones had been heaped along the route at the halfway point, Craigton, and with no time to take evasive action, the crew of the approaching carriage could only watch in horror as their vehicle hit the pile. With what must have been a terrifying noise, one of the fragile wooden wheels collapsed, sending the top-heavy carriage rolling onto its side, killing four passengers and one of the men in charge of the engine. An investigation proved inconclusive but the deed was done, patronage waned, and the service ceased operation soon after.

Betty Boothroyd, then Speaker of the House, rides alongside Lord Montagu on his father's 1899 Daimler as they enter Palace Yard, Westminster to celebrate the centenary of the 1896 Emancipation Run (see page 59).

Yet, it took another thirty years for the British government to impose a law that specifically targeted road locomotives. The Locomotives on Highways Act was passed by Parliament in 1861 and, for the first time, introduced a road tax for self-propelled vehicles. It placed regulations on the minimum width of a traction engine's wheels ensuring weight was spread over a wide area, and enforced tolls per tonnage of load carried in any wagons pulled behind. It also placed a 10mph speed limit on open roads and 5mph in inhabited areas.

In 1865, the rules were amended with the 'Red Flag Act', which specified that all traction engines should only be operated on the highway with a crew of no fewer than three. Before then, a vehicle of this type could be driven by just the engineman and steersman, but from 1865, there needed to be a third person carrying a red flag, and walking at least

The 1860 Rickett steam carriage, owned by the Earl of Caithness. Builder Thomas Rickett is at the rear, attending to the fire.

60 yards ahead. Their job was to give notice to other road users of the approaching locomotive and assist with the passage of horses or horse-drawn carriages. The 10mph maximum speed limit was reduced, and for the next thirty years it remained at 4mph in rural areas, and a tediously slow 2mph, or walking pace, in built-up areas.

By the 1890s, attitudes towards the motor car were changing, and supporters in Britain were vigorously campaigning to revise outdated legislation. It all came to a

Henry Knight's 1895 Knight tricycle in its later rebuilt form as a four-wheeler.

head in October 1895, when wealthy entrepreneur John Henry Knight stood alongside his assistant James Pullinger before a Farnham magistrates' court and was found guilty of using a locomotive without a licence and without a man with a red flag walking in front. The vehicle in question was an almost silent-running lightweight tricycle of Knight's own design, and the attention the case attracted when

reported in the press publicly highlighted the injustice of the conviction.

Crowds line the route at Reigate in Surrey during the 1896 'Emancipation Run', an event organised to celebrate new laws that lifted restrictions on motoring.

Parliament had habitually taken a hard line on mechanised road transport largely due to the fact many Members had personally invested heavily in the railways. But even they were starting to look kindly on the plight of the autocarist, especially as a motoring obsession was growing among many of their own peers. In 1896, MPs debated a new Locomotives on Highways Bill with a view to placing vehicles of less than three tons' unladen weight in a separate category of 'light locomotives', and disposing of the crew of three and the man with the red flag rules. The bill was passed, and those owning automobiles could now enjoy unaccompanied open-road motoring at a new speed limit, a heady 14mph!

To mark this momentous turning point, Harry J. Lawson, founder of the Daimler Motor Company Limited, gathered together friends, associates and members of the recently formed Motor Car Club at Charing Cross Hotel on the morning of 14 November 1896. After a sumptuous breakfast during

A 1902 Darracq
at the 2007
London to
Brighton Veteran
Car Run.

which a red flag was unceremoniously torn in half by Lord
Winchelsea, thirty or so cars set off from the Metropole Hotel
and drove in celebration from London to the seaside town of
Brighton. Lawson promoted the event as the 'Emancipation
Run' as he felt motorists had finally been set free from the
antiquated and inappropriate rules laid down in Locomotive
Acts over a quarter of a century before, legislation that most
certainly should not have applied to his fellow autocarists.

Although there seemed to be an air of increasing leniency
within Parliament when it came to the subject of governing
the highways, there were still some issues that needed to be

A 1904 De-Dion
Bouton and a
1903 Rambler at
the start of the
2005 London to
Brighton Veteran
Car Run.

A 1903 Stanley steam car makes a swift getaway from Hyde Park at the start of the 2007 London to Brighton Veteran Car Run.

addressed. In 1898, John Douglas-Scott-Montagu, MP for the New Forest, attempted to drive his 12hp Daimler through the gates of Palace Yard. The police on guard, however, prevented his entry most likely due to its excessive exhaust emissions. Other MPs had gained access on previous occasions, but in electric vehicles, and Montagu was forced to abandon his car outside. He refused to let the dispute lie, the episode made the headlines, and soon after the authorities sent an apology with permission for him to use the yard in future. In 1998, his son Edward, Lord Montagu of Beaulieu, commemorated the 100th anniversary of this historic event using the same car. This time, he ensured there would be no objection, taking Speaker of the House, Betty Boothroyd, along for the ride!

Although many local authorities stubbornly refused to recognise the 14mph ruling laid down in 1896, imposing a 12mph limit instead, the law was changed once again in 1903 with the Motor Car Act, whereby the maximum speed was raised to 20mph.

In 1927, the Emancipation Run was re-enacted, attracting a similar number of cars as on that first occasion in 1896.

Probably the best-known veteran car of all is this 1904 Darracq, which featured in the film *Genevieve*.

Thereafter, it became a yearly fixture in the motoring calendar until the outbreak of the Second World War, which resulted in an eight-year interlude. Once hostilities in Europe had ended, thoughts turned once again to resurrecting the event, and since 1947, the London to Brighton Veteran Car Run has been held on every first Sunday in November. Starting from Hyde Park, the modern day London to Brighton Veteran Car Run takes a route across Westminster Bridge, down through south London and then out onto the old A23. After an official coffee stop in Crawley, it makes a last push over the South Downs, culminating on Madeira Drive, overlooking the sea at Brighton. The trials and tribulations of those who make the 54-mile journey year on year were immortalised in the 1953 feature film *Genevieve*, starring a 1904 Darracq, John Gregson, Kenneth More, Dinah Sheridan and Kay Kendall.

Over the years, well-known names from the world of motoring and motor racing, showbiz personalities and even royalty have numbered among the participants. Today, hundreds of vehicles take part in the race, which is open to all eligible 'veteran' cars built up to and including 31 December 1904, those registered after that date falling into the next category of the 'Edwardian' era. But that's another story!

FURTHER READING

Bennett, Elizabeth. *Thousand Mile Trial.* Elizabeth Bennett, 2000.

Burgess-Wise, David. *Brighton Belles: A Celebration of Veteran Cars.* Crowood Press, 2006.

Collins, Paul and Stratton, Michael. *British Car Factories from 1896: A Complete Historical, Geographical, Architectural & Technological Survey.* Veloce Publishing, 1993.

Edwards, Michael. *De Dion Bouton: An Illustrated Guide to Type & Specification 1899–1904.* Surrenden Press, 2016.

Edwards, Michael. *The Tricycle Book: 1895–1902 Part One.* Surrenden Press, 2018.

Flower, Raymond and Wynn Jones, Michael. *One Hundred Years of Motoring: An RAC Social History of the Car.* RAC Publishing, 1981.

Georgano, G.N., Baldwin, Nick, Clausager, Anders and Wood, Jonathan. *Britain's Motor Industry: The First Hundred Years.* G.T. Foulis & Co., 1995.

Hylton, Stuart. *The Horseless Carriage: The Birth of the Motor Age.* The History Press, 2009.

Kimberly, Damien. *Coventry's Motorcar Heritage.* The History Press, 2012.

Lynch, Brendan. *Green Dust: Ireland's Unique Motor Racing History, 1900–1939.* Portobello Publishing, 1988.

Lynch, Brendan. *Triumph of the Red Devil: The Irish Gordon Bennett Cup Race 1903.* Portobello Publishing, 2002.

Montagu, Lord and Burgess-Wise, David. *Daimler Century: The Full History of Britain's Oldest Car Maker.* Patrick Stephens Ltd, 1995.

Montgomery, Bob. *The 1903 Irish Gordon Bennett: The Race that Saved Motor Sport.* Bookmarque Publishing, 2000.

Nicholson, T.R. *The Birth of the British Motor Car, 1769–1897 (Volume 1: A new machine 1769–1842;*

Volume 2: Revival and defeat 1842–1893; Volume 3: The last battle 1894–1897). Macmillan, 1982.
Ware, Michael E. *Making of the Motor Car, 1895–1930.* Moorland Publishing, 1976.

PLACES TO VISIT

Atwell-Wilson Motor Museum, Stockley Lane, Calne, Wiltshire SN11 0NF. Telephone: 01249 813119. Website: www.atwellwilson.org.uk

Beamish Museum, Beamish, County Durham DH9 0RG. Telephone: 0191 370 4000. Website: www.beamish.org.uk

Black Country Living Museum, Tipton Road, Dudley, West Midlands DY1 4SQ. Telephone: 0121 557 9643. Website: www.bclm.co.uk

British Motor Museum, Banbury Road, Gaydon, Warwickshire CV35 0BJ. Telephone: 01926 641188. Website: www.britishmotormuseum.co.uk

Brooklands Museum, Brooklands Road, Weybridge, Surrey KT13 0SL. Telephone: 01932 857381. Website: www.brooklandsmuseum.com

Cotswold Motoring Museum & Toy Collection, Bourton-on-the-Water, Gloucestershire GL54 2BY. Telephone: 01451 821255. Website: www.cotswoldmotoringmuseum.co.uk

Coventry Transport Museum, Millennium Place, Hales Street, Coventry, Warwickshire CV1 1JD. Telephone: 02476 234270. Website: www.transport-museum.com

Glasgow Life, 38 Albion Street, Glasgow G1 1LH. Telephone: 0141 287 4350. Website: www.glasgowlife. org.uk/museums/collections#transport-and-technology-1

Haynes International Motor Museum, Sparkford, Yeovil, Somerset BA22 7LH. Telephone: 01963 440804. Website: www.haynesmotormuseum.com

Lakeland Motor Museum Ltd, Old Blue Mill, Backbarrow, Ulverston, Cumbria LA12 8TA. Telephone: 01539 530400. Website: www.lakelandmotormuseum.co.uk

Milestones Museum, Leisure Park, Churchill Way West, Basingstoke, Hampshire RG22 6PG. Telephone: 01256 639550. Website: www.milestonesmuseum.org.uk

The National Motor Museum, Beaulieu, New Forest, Hampshire SO42 7ZN. Telephone: 01590 612345. Website: www.beaulieu.co.uk

Science Museum, Exhibition Road, South Kensington, London SW7 2DD. Telephone: 0333 241 4000 (020 7942 4000). Website: www.sciencemuseum.org.uk

Streetlife Museum, High Street, Hull, HU1 1PS. Telephone: 01482 300300. Website: www.hcandl.co.uk/ museums-and-galleries/streetlife-museum

A 1902 Wolseley four-cylinder.

INDEX

Page numbers in bold refer to illustrations.